LETTER FROM THE EDITORS

    The world is a cruel place, the people in it even crueler. Such is the reality we must face, must live with. But what if we made it better? What if naming our demons and crying out our pains healed our souls and the land we walk on for future generations? This rejection of what has been handed to us by our ancestors and our earthly peers is what makes reality bearable.

    REJECTING REALITY isn't just about the fantastic and other worldly, it's also about what the now and what will be. It's about daring to be different and daring to be bold in the face of people who aim to keep the status quo. Fall apart if you must, leave your community behind if you need to, go insane if that's what it takes: do something to bear the burden of living. Find your god and your sanity in places you've been too scared to venture into, just like we did in these pages.

    Once you find your own version of heaven or pick up the crumbling pieces of your sanity in order to become a stronger version of yourself. We only ask that you share this strength, this heaven, this happiness and this hopeful present with the person next to you. It may be a friend who is struggling with facing their own reality or a sister who is fighting her own demons. Help them find the light of hope and bravery to break down the walls of their current hell.

    In a world where everyone is so caught up with their own troubles and cries for help, we sometimes fail to take action to make a better reality for ourselves and others. Rip off the blindfold that is covering the harsh truth and run.

    If you get tired, then write, scream or be the shoulder your friend needs. Don't keep the sweet taste of making a better reality to yourself. Share that joy with others and continue to break down the status quo. Inspire your friends, loved ones or strangers so they too can create a reality that is safe, happy and hopeful.

    At the end of the day that's all we strive to have and be. But before you can do that, you need to do it for yourself. Once you finish these magical yet painfully truthful pieces, we hope you find courage and gather your strength to create a safer present for yourself. Abandon that hurtful kingdom you call home and fight the orange ogres in your life with your words and magic. Remember that you are not alone. You are not the only one stuck in this cruel reality. You are not the only one fighting the good fight.

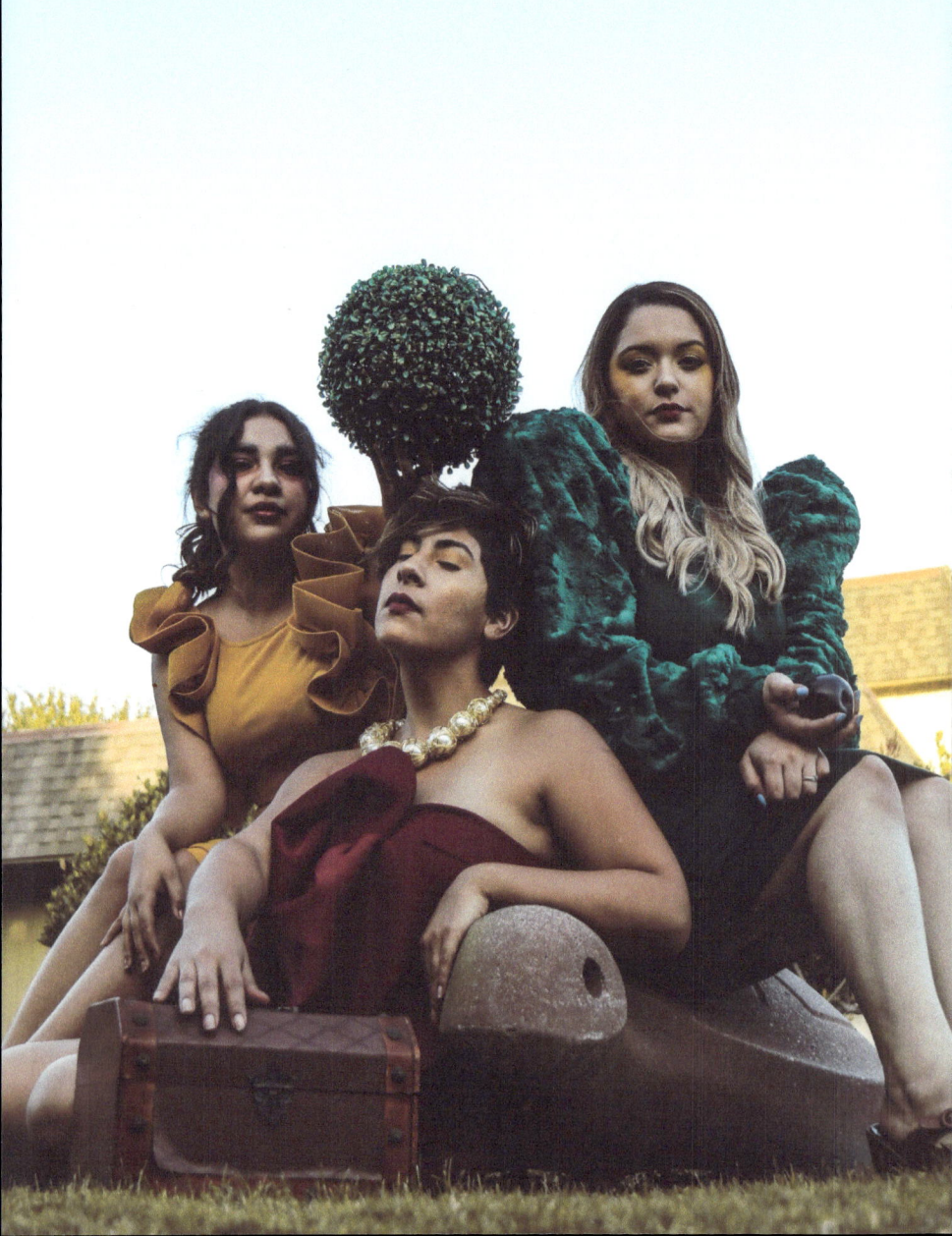

THIS MONTH

- 5 LAS TRES BRUJAS
- 9 WOOD & AIR: A SESTINA
- 10 LA JUNGLA
- 11 HALLOW'S END
- 15 HANG HER ON THE CLOTHESLINE
- 17 GRINGOLANDIA
- 20 DEAR GOD
- 23 CASA
- 24 THEY SENT ME TO HELL, SHE SENT ME TO MYSELF
- 28 ANCIENT TIGER
- 29 MAKING ROOM
- 31 ASI TU ME MATAS
- 32 HOW DO I GET RID OF THE HURT
- 35 PRINCIPITO

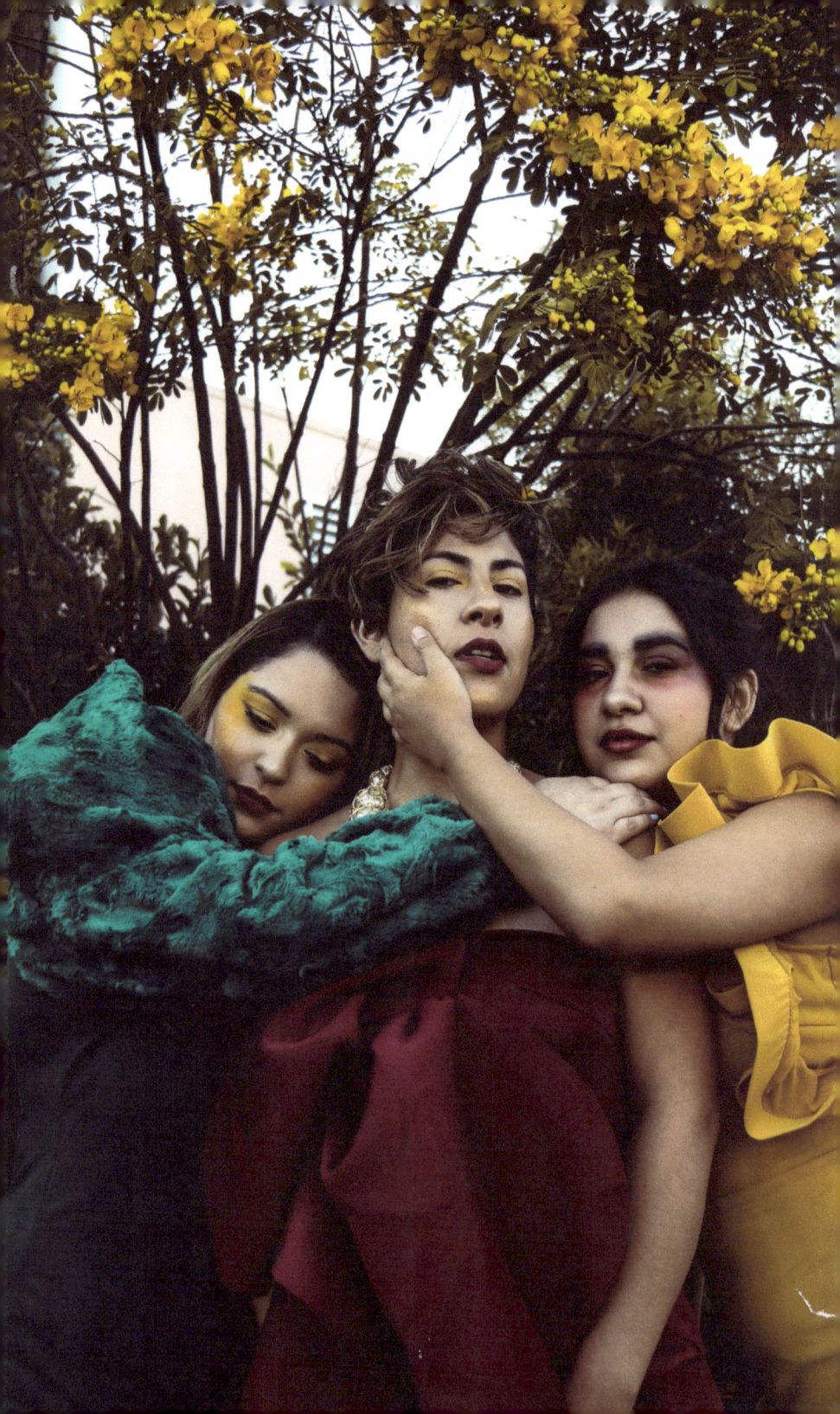

LAS TRES BRUJAS

BRENDA HERNÁNDEZ JAIMES

The residents of Villa de los Lobos called them the daughters of the devil. Three young and unmarried women who spoke in tongues and dressed themselves as eccentric birds could definitely not be God's children. The sky had turned purple and the air smelled of plums the day the strange women had arrived to the small and colonial pueblo mágico. Their arrival may have gone unnoticed if it were not for the rattle of the bells of the ancient baroque church. The devoted and mustios residents swarmed out of the large wooden doors and encountered their new neighbors.

Had it not been for the well respected mayor of Villa de los Lobos, claiming to be their uncle, the persignados residents would have burned the young women alive. Nevertheless, rumors began to circulate that Cosima, Aura and Neoma Ruano were not virtuous women. Forced smiles would encounter the three sisters and daggers filled with lies would be pierced painlessly through their backs.

Bitter mothers held their sons and daughters close while whispering lies into their ears. It was said that they gave their bodies to men and turned them into stone turtles. These ludicrous lies reached the sisters but they never seemed affected by the hexes. If the residents of Villa de los Lobos had ever taken a moment to speak to the young women, they would have learned that their hexes were no match compared to the dark curses that had tortured them back in their homeland.

For Cosima, Aura and Neoma had escaped the claws of war and the living nightmares that had taken their parents away from them. The hell that they had lived in was nothing compared to what the close minded residents of Villa de los Lobos thought of them. This small pueblo mágico was their new home and their gift to live without fear.

Freedom tasted sweet, gone was the sour taste and rotting smell of war. Their wands had been destroyed by the foreign invaders, but they had learned the pure magic of their ancestors. Wands weren't required when Quetzalcóatl was the prince of the nahuales. Their grandmother had taught them wandless magic, to cast charms and heal those in need. It was only fitting to continue their traditions in their new home.

In Villa de los Lobos the three witches created their own new life and transformed the pueblo mágico into their vital refuge. A place where they could live in peace and unleash their incredible magic without fear of restraint. A reality that was filled with hope and happiness. A present and future that filled their aura with warmth.

Even though their home was a welcomed haven, their hearts were heavy with homesickness. Memories of their childhood and of their people filled their soul.

Mist clouded their future. Would they ever go back to their sweet home? Would they embrace their people and build up the pieces that were destroyed? Only time would tell. Meanwhile the only way for them to help the future of their home was to enrich their minds. To become the best witches they could be in order to reconstruct their home.

War had exiled the three sisters, but it had also reunited them. Their sisterly bond had become stronger and caused their magic to delve deeper in ways that would have not been possible beforehand.

Cosima, who was the oldest had discovered her inner eye. Bits and pieces of the past would appear when she would bite into the plums that grew in her uncle's garden. History of her people would become clear and past tragedies reminded her that they had always been strong. When she poured honey into her cranberry tea, muddled prophecies filled her thoughts. She would feel cold as ice, but the strength of past nightmares would poke through her soul. They would get through this.

Aura found peace with her potions. Happiness filled her veins as she chopped mandrake leaves and grinded them with plums and bat fangs in her molcajete. She would send her potions to the broken friends that had escaped from their homeland. With a few sips of the tranquility potion, they would be able to sleep without being tormented by nightmares. But she would never take her own remedy. She was persistent of never forgetting the past. The dark past was the fuel she needed to go on and mend her people even if it robbed of her sleep at night.

Neoma was the youngest and the most gifted. She had inherited the most extraordinary gift that her ancestors were known for. Back in her homeland she had discovered she was a nahual. Before the war, her mother had begun to prepare her to take her true form. She had discovered that she had been blessed by the great Huitzilopochtli himself. Neoma had only flown once as a hummingbird, but once the blood began to spill in her land it seemed her gift was no more. With Aura's potion and the peace that filled Villa de los Lobos, Neoma began to sing short and soft calls in hopes that a friend or loved one would hear her call and find them.

Hurtful lies continued to seep into the cobbled streets of Villa de los Lobos, but the sisters never dwelled on powerless words. They had faced a much darker force that had not destroyed them. Words could strip away truth, but bloody actions take away life.

The three witches could only live and thrive in the freedom that this pueblo mágico bestowed on them. It may have not been a perfect world, but Cosima, Aura and Neoma were able to unbind themselves from the claws of death for just a moment. They waited and prepared themselves for the day was near when they would trample their enemies with their knowledge and strength. They owed it to their people to make a life by what fate had given them and to give as much life in return. For one day and that day was near, the three witches needed to be ready to take on the orange monster that had turned their nightmares into reality.

EDITORIAL SHOOT
Models: Anabel Orozco, Annette Cortez & Brenda Deshazer
Photographer: Josephine Jael Jimenez
Stylist: Brenda Hernández Jaimes
Makeup: Anabel Orozco, Annette Cortez, Josephine Jael Jimenez

WOOD AND AIR: A SESTINA

LORRAINE RUMSON

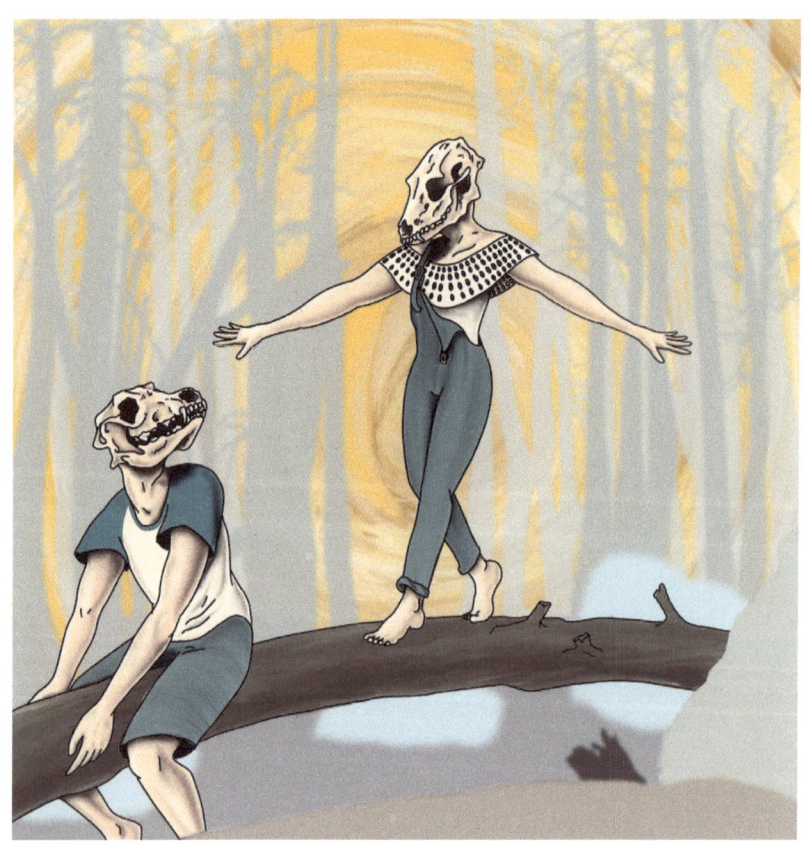

UNTITLED
Digital Illustration *by Bryn Riihimaki*

The sky cracks open, and the eastern air
Comes pouring in like water from a spring.
I welcome it. I grow up tall like grass
And stretch my arms across the firewood
To draw a drop of February sun.
Your shadow in the distance gives me pause.

Between the trees, across the bank, you pause,
Look back on me, and something in the air
Turns summer. Look across, the easing sun
Has made it easy for me, now, in spring,
To jump the creek. I leave your home-safe wood
And leave my foot-marks in the peeping grass.

I follow you; each muffled blade of grass
Protects me from your wife, who might me pause
To see me leave behind my work: bread, wood,
And other mundane daily work. The air
Lifts back a curl threatening to spring
And make me indecent beneath the sun.

"Where are you going?" Buck moth in the sun,
You flit away. I follow through the grass,
Up higher than my waist. I hear the spring
Disturb your crossing, so I do not pause
But feel your presence closer in the air.
Until, when we are sheltered in the wood,
You come clear, leaning, hand upon the wood,
Your back to me. You're blotted from the sun
With heavy uncut branches, heavy air,
And heavy silence, broken by the grass
That rustles all around me, and I pause
With one foot on each border of the spring.
"Come closer, dear thing." So I cross the spring,
I grip the tree beside you, feel the wood,
Warm underneath my hand; the pause
Unbroken. Your eyes look darker in the sun.
We are alone. No rustle in the grass.
No village, nothing; you, me, and the air.

The pause will leave me face-first in the spring.
You turn to air, and I'm left in the wood,
With your trees, and the sunlight on the grass.

LA JUNGLA

CARLOS GARCÍA LEÓN

My time in the jungle has been filled with
the silence before a killing.
It's a weird jungle, rules by two houses
with lots of ancestry;
Roots that run deep with pride
and thick with blood.

The Bears are a large family
because the generations before me
had many cubs
for cultural and land reasons,
but the name comes from reasons unknown.

It has been said that the bears were Garcías
before the transformation
that began when animals started growing
from inside the beast that walked on two feet
and many other animals came too.

Like the Lions, who came from the Leóns,
they were equally a big family, but independent too.
Only meeting a few times a year,
but always having fun when it happened.
Their kill has always been slow.

I am a hybrid of the two
Not uncommon, however not on top
of the food chain that powered these beasts.
Yet, my strength doesn't come from my pack,
but from the solitude that comes from
analyzing your patterns, and your weakness.

All pure species have them,
the things that ruin the herd,
make it easy to slaughter the house
and I have those secrets vested in me.

Us hybrids are only waiting
to bring the poison to your rules
to weaken the bonds that hold you together
and finally have some peace in our kingdom.

HALLOW'S END

CHASE GOLDSMITH

There were only vast fields of dirt. Occasionally there was an animal that passed by, a farm or factory. The one thing that never seemed to change out here was the oppressing sun. It was beautiful to see something too old and expansive, it brought about a feeling of cal…

"We have a half a tank of gas," I said.

"Well what if there is no gas station for awhile," said Sofie.

"Honey, relax we are going to be fine, we have at least 25 miles before the gas gets too low and town is 10 miles away, we'll be fine."

I knew that wasn't enough for her, she would rather be…

"I'd rather be safe than sorry."

If it is unclear, my girlfriend is slightly, well…

"It would really make me less nervous if we got the gas, it's only $50."

"Honey don't worry we'll be fine, just enjoy the scenery of this old dusty desert."

"There's the gas station coming up, please lets go."

"No, we're going to be fine. Please stop, you are bugging the hell out of me."

As we approached the town we saw it's sign appear on an old wood sign, 'Hallows End' and for sure, Sofie would get nervous.

"This place really gives me the hebe jebbes."

"I need you to relax, between the gas and this, you really are getting on my nerves."

Sofie's face turned a little pale and turned away from me.

"Sorry, I'll leave you alone."

We hopped off the old asphalt road and onto the older dirt path. This road was riddled with rocks, causing the car to rumble and rattle. As we approached the town the shaking seemed to get worse.

"Please slow down! You are going to total the car" shrieked Sofie.

"This is too much fun and the car will be fine it has some kick ass shocks."

The shaking kept increasing until a giant bump in the road threw us up into the air. The car landed softly, making us feel uncomfortable. But I was not going to add to Sofie's anxiety.

"We did it, we are now in the threshold of Hallows End," I said.

"Oh my God, you can no longer drive anymore."

The entire town sat on a single road and as we drove down it we noticed that the town seemed dead. Ahead we saw a building that read INN and we decided to go inside to see if there was anyone in the deserted town.

"Are you sure we should be here, it's so spooky" said Sofie.

"Don't worry so much, we are just going in to look and see if there is anyone here and if there isn't, we will leave."

To be honest I did feel afraid, this place gave me a weird feeling, but I needed to be brave for her.

We entered the tall towering inn, the inside was just as empty as the town outside; all the furniture inside was as brown as the exterior with tables and wood chairs in front of a long bar table that stretched the length of the back wall. On the table was the most exquisite thing, a bright bronze bell that had a sign that read 'Ring For Service.'

"Look there's a bell. I'll ring it and see if there is anyone here that can help us okay," I said.

"No don't something bad is going to happen, please don't do it."

"Please don't worry, I need you to relax, there's probably no one here."

I sprang towards the bell and rang it three times...silence, I rang it again for good measure... nothing.

"I guess there is no one here," I said as I turned towards Sofie.

"Did you need something folks?" said a voice from behind.

The hairs on my neck became icicles I turned around to see who it was.

It was a man who seemed to be in his late 60's, with an upper lip mustache and thinning hair, clothed in an old suit.

His sudden presence sent me into a shock and Sofie let out a scream.

"When did you get here?" I said.

"Never mind you that, I am here to offer you help."

"I just want to know where we are and where is some gas?"

His eyes flashed red and he gave me a subtle smirk.

"Well I think I may be able to help. This is a very old place with even older traditions. As for your gas we have a supply just in the back, I can grab some for you folks, but first would either of you like a drink?"

"No" said Sofie and I together.

"Please I insist. You two look positively thirsty."

From under the bar table he took out two delicious looking drinks.

"Well I am pretty thirsty," said Sofie.

"Here enjoy your drink."

As soon as she went for the drink he grabbed her by the hand and a devilish look came upon his face. Then the two of them disappeared.

At first I thought that this was all a dream and that I should wake any second... but I was still there in that damned dusty den.

"I must thank you for coming here, we were looking for a couple of your age," said a voice from behind.

"Where is she?"

"Don't worry you can see her but only if you perform one task for me."

"What are you?"

"That is not your concern, your Sofie is what you should worry about."

"What do you want?"
"Drink this poison or leave this town and never look back."
"What? No, how will this do anything at all?"
"If you drink it you can see Sofie, if not leave."
"And you will let her go?"
"Yes we will free her."
"Fine!"
"Here you go, drink up."
That same devilish smile crept upon his face and he presented me with a bronzed cup. I drank the contents of the drink in one large gulp.
"Now where is she?"
"Here"
I turned around and the room was full of people and they were all looking at me.
"The children of the sacrament have come and we will be free!" said the bartender.
"Where is Sofie?"
"Behind you."
As I turned my legs gave out and I hit the floor. The poison was working, I saw Sofie tied up with rope on a stake.
"I love you Sofie and I am so sorry I did this to us, at least you can be free."
"I love you t…"
The bartender stopped her short as he had taken her heart.
"Here is the heart of the sacrifice, now we shall light the flame and burn together the two children of sacrament."
This was my end, at least I get to die next to the one I loved.

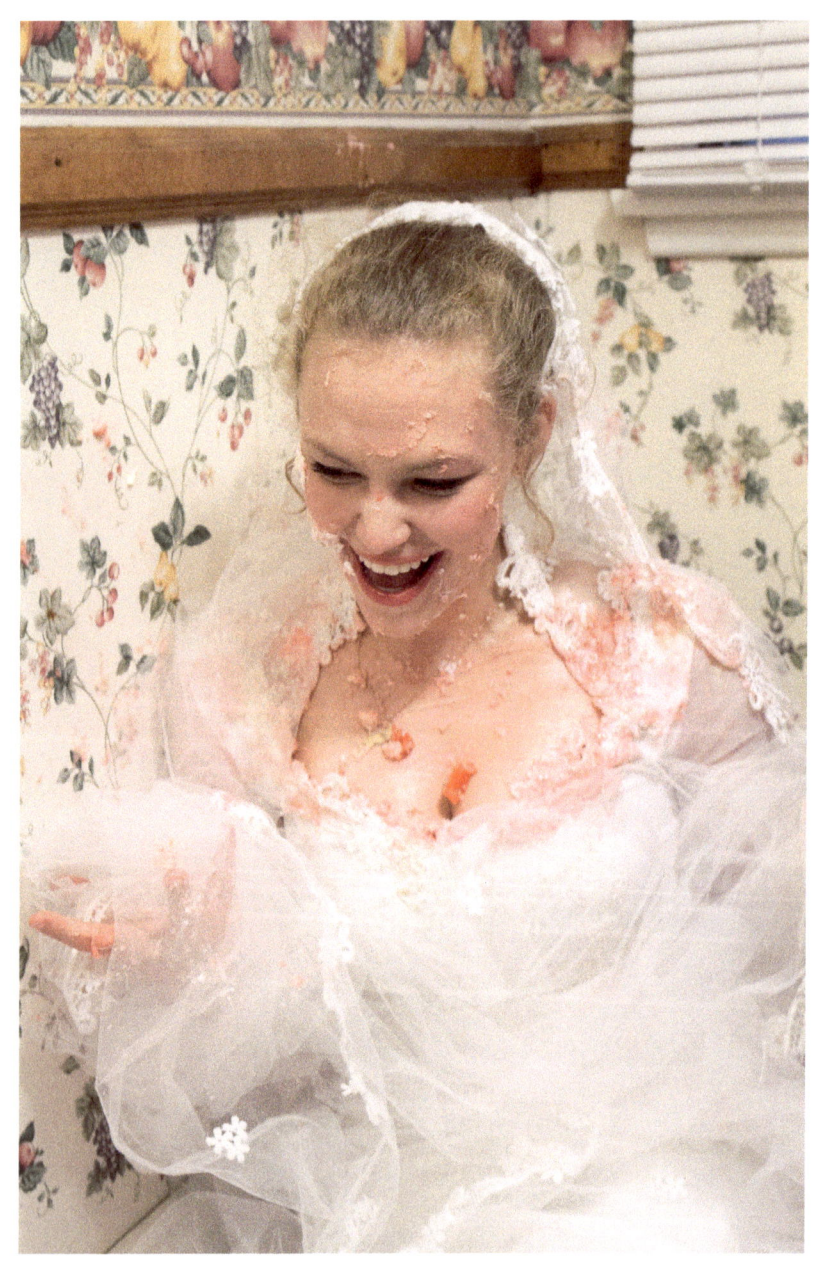

Hang her on the clothesline,
set her out to dry.
We've washed her,
bathed her,
scalded off her sin.
Let her hang in the breeze
to rest for a while
before we use her again
and soil her skin
only to wash her over and over.

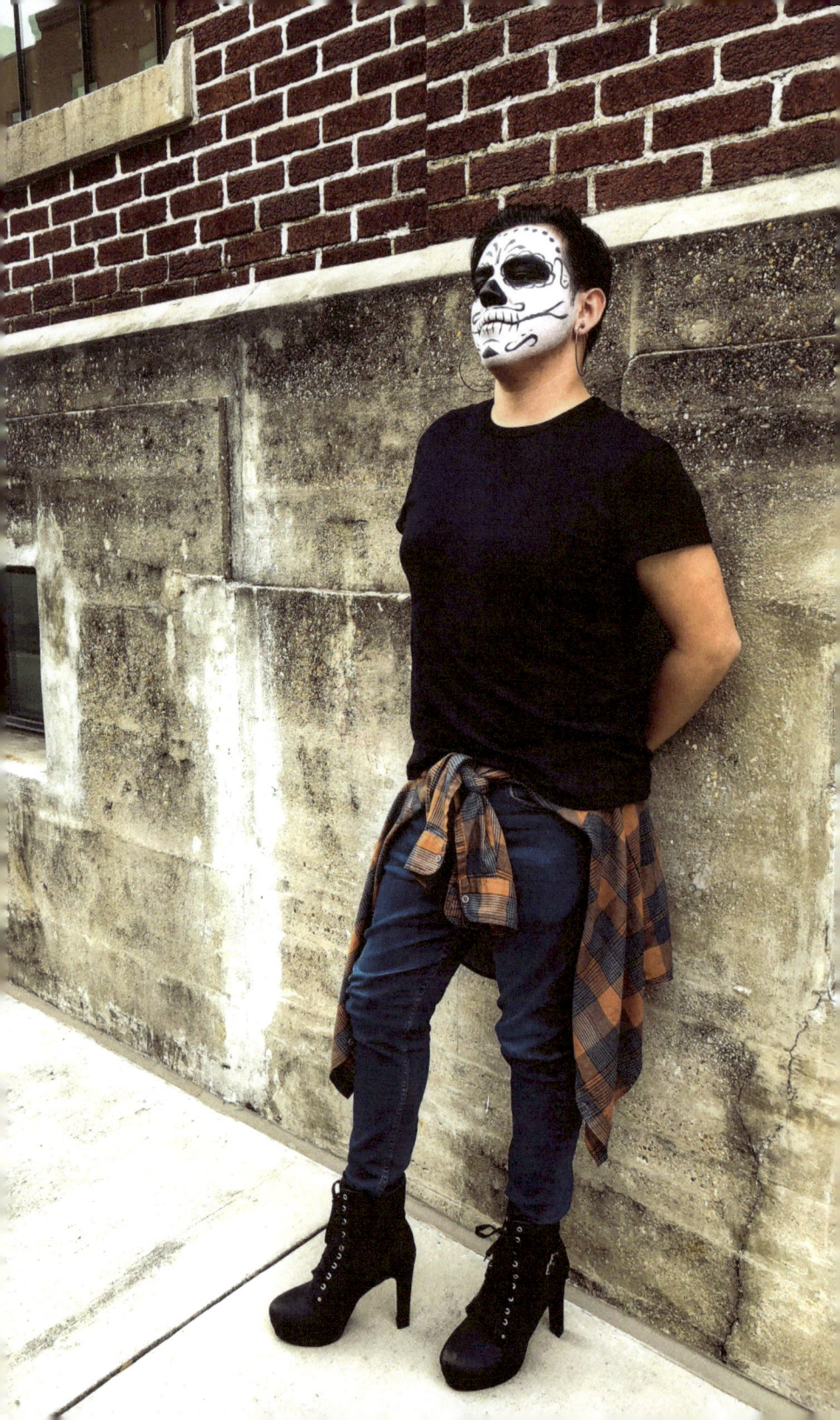

GRINGOLANDIA

JOSEPH A. REYES

For mi gente, mi familia
Ultimate resistance grounds you
Create a world where you shine
Know that you own yourself

Whiteness has created false reality
Hoping to gain control over our us
Instead, they've liberated our resistance
Try try try all you want, Gringolandia
Estamos aqui, we are the first inhabitants

Sing your hopes to the stars
Unique tongues bring
Praise to the indigenous ancestors
Relish in your beautiful, brown skin
Embrace el sol and Mother Earth
Make the American dream your bitch by
Announcing your everlasting presence
Celebrate tu vida every damn day
You are a tree giving life to the future

Photograph *by Joseph A. Reyes*

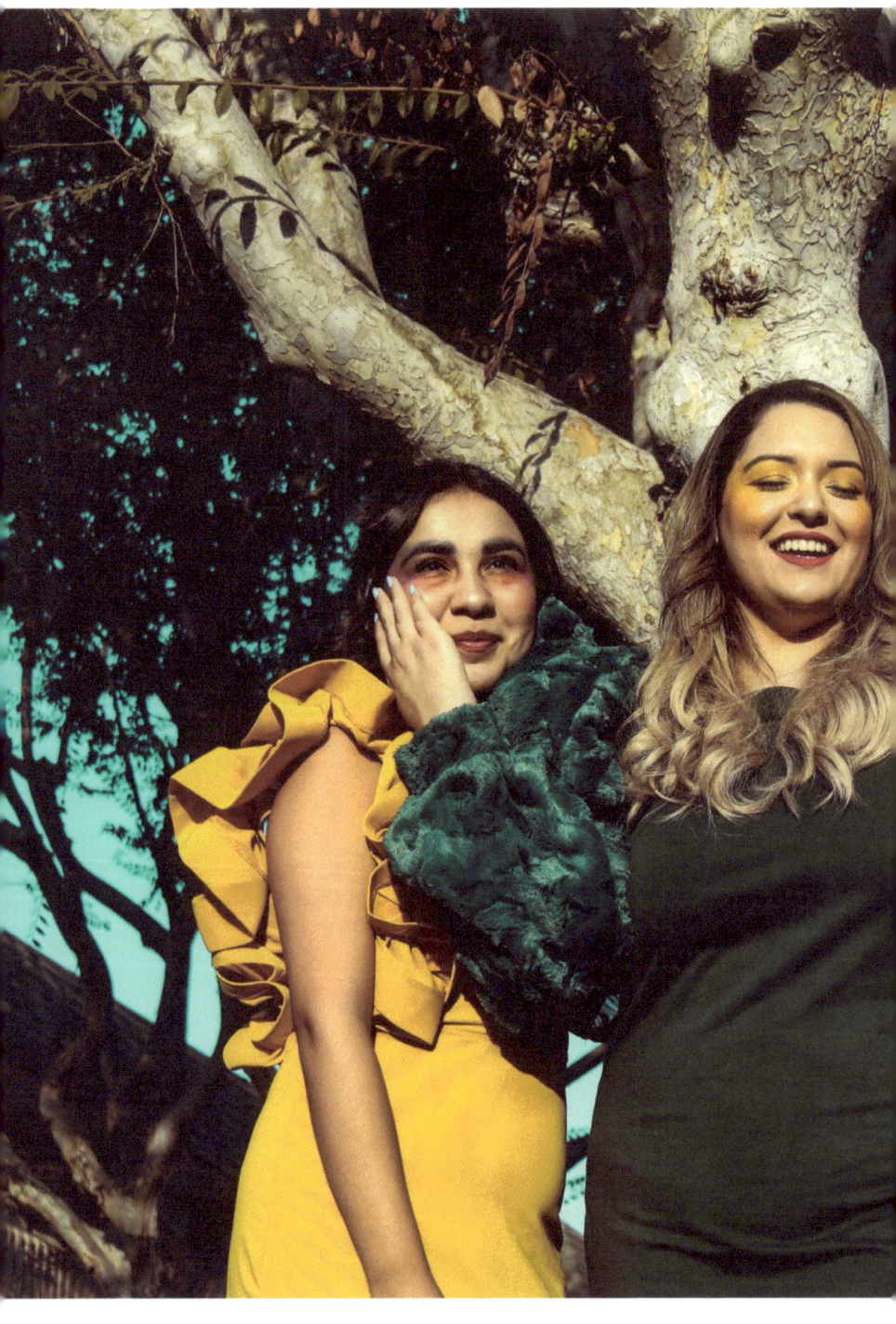

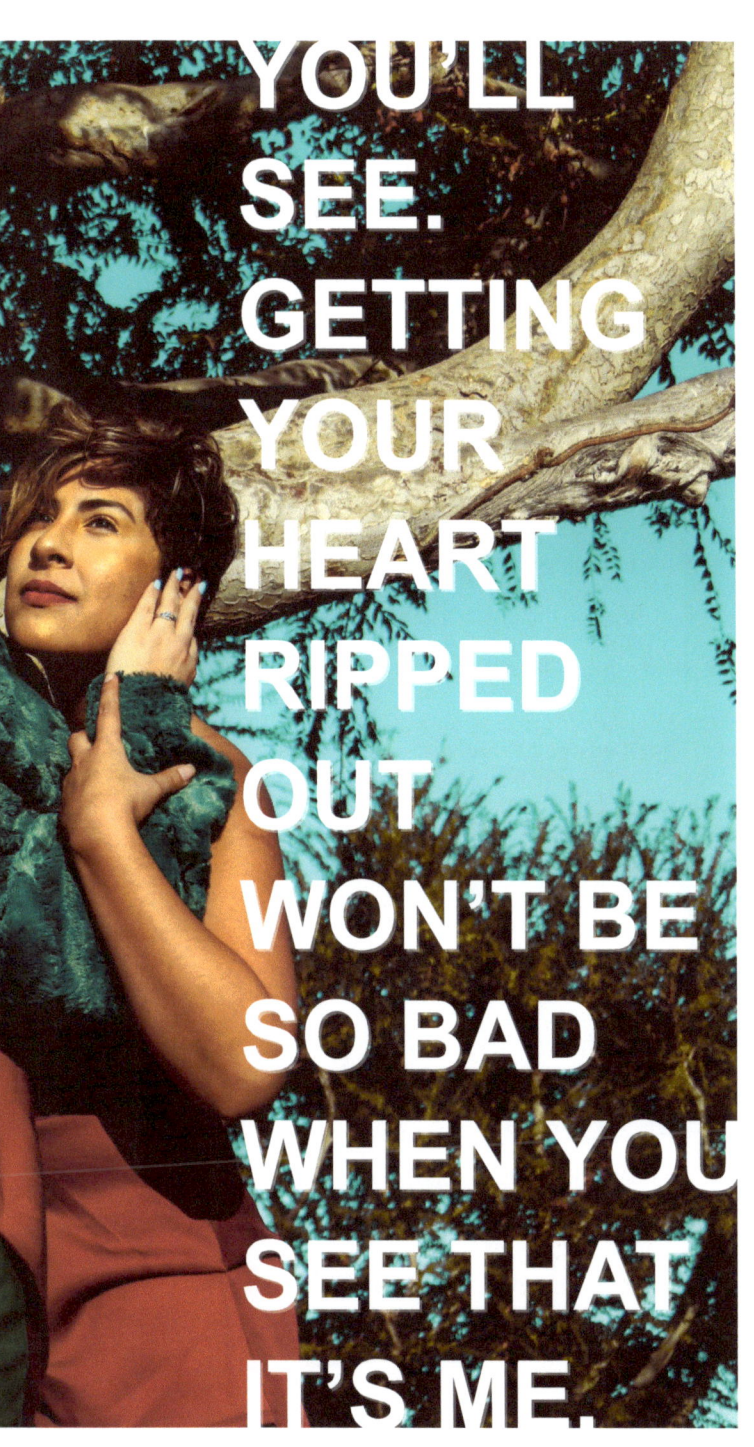

DEAR GOD
EROS PURIZAGA

god, you bid me come be honest, well then let's talk cause here i am.
there are so many things to pray for
& i don't even have the heart to give a damn.

but I'm here per your request,
so i know that i must care at least a little.
a human with a heart of mould; it's life's unceasing riddle.

although, i do sometimes feel as if i ask way too many questions.
but i know you know i know
i want to align with your perception.

should i start off by praying for myself or praying for others,
should i follow my mind or my heart?
or should i follow all of the life path numbers on my numerology chart?

& where, when, & how does my soul come in to play?
do controversial questions lead me to you, lead me with you,
or lead me astray?

when will i ever learn to sit still?
& when & if i do will i then learn
how to control my free will?

you tell me come be perfect,
but you know very well that I can't.
you say to come humbly & speak to you of it, but it feels like i rant.

i've heard some say that it's the numb ones
who feel you the deepest & who know you the best.
yet sometimes it seems as if it's the dumb ones
that treat you the cheapest whom you've chosen to bless.

or what about the ones who are too afraid to trust
because they don't want to get hurt.
so they proceed to go about their time speaking of other people's dirt.

but that very statement is so ironic, why did you design us like that?
& it also looks as if we're all born hyper-hedonic
& make up our own subjective facts.

sometimes i feel like i'm too smart to go to church.
it's hard enough to burn off deadwood in your life
& organize when all of your blessings come with a curse.

maybe i just have a reckless passion,
but i know you know i know that my intentions
are to speak the truthest truth, no matter what the fucking damage.

cause if i care too much what people think, i'll never achieve my purpose.
no one would ever hear my truest of thoughts
& would only experience my surface.

& sometimes i think you sound like wishful thinking, if i'm honest.
you say to seek you earnestly,
but our very questions you admonish.

sometimes my skepticism feels like it's my one true love.
but i can't help but to even question
your seemingly poorly-designed unceasing mental drudge.

what was the fruit in the garden? was it the means by which we speak?
was it the knowledge of your bargain,
the double-edged sword that we might've unsheathed?

god, did you choose me? i cannot stand the uncertainty,
but i guess i understand it's place.
god, i seek you earnestly. you've designed me to disagree,
yet simultaneously seek your face.

i'm out to seek how much influence i really have on this earth.
if not, then tell me, god, i beg you,
how does a human ever find their worth?

feeling like I got something to say, but who am i to say it?
i don't know if someone controls the game,
but i honestly sometimes i just don't want to play it.

sometimes i feel like i inspire myself, but is that really just you in me?
i think i'm starting to believe everyone has a divine spark
but am i only entertaining blasphemy?

because if everyone has a divine spark,
will it reunite with you in heaven?
if not, then god, i'm sure no one will surely get in.

cause we're all a little more selfish than someone else,
we're also all a little more lovely too.
but who am i to judge or even have any opinions,
when the one who should be ruling should be you?

i'm torn between worm and god, but i appreciate the tearing.
everyday the struggle is to contemplate whether or not
that very burden is worth bearing.

i know you tell us not to doubt & if we didn't that our faith would be perfect.
but my doubts feel like they only get me closer to you,
so if doubts are sin, then it seems worth it

but aren't you the giver of my faith,
so have we all been doomed from the start?
tell me is it really you who's in charge of softening & hardening hearts?

they say trust the voice of god, but it feels we got too many in my head
& i've heard some people say
life is whatever wolf that you keep well fed.

& then they call it lukewarm, but some may refer to it as balance.
the more my curiosity leads me closer to you,
the more they say i am calloused.

but who are they to even speak into what i believe about you?
some of them keep their darkest thoughts at bay,
& some even do the same thing with you.

yet, why does it feel wrong when i mention others sins
in my day to day prayers?
cause isn't that how karma works?
their sins affect my world & mine affect theirs.

some have said that i think too much,
yet i feel i don't think enough.
i always feel like i'm just living life confidently insecure in existential bluff.

they tell me to be myself, but i don't know why, weirdly, that scares me.
maybe it's because when i am, my faith is compromised,
although you already know this, clearly, you made me.

faithful doubt, or doubtful faith? idk, guess i'll be good for goodness sake.
to find you, it feels closely far.
but i know you know i know that i just want to be where you are.

here i go again ranting & ranting like i always do.
but i know you know i know that i'm just sitting here trying
to know you like you know me too.

CASA

CARLOS GARCÍA LEÓN

Kissing sin always felt so so so good.
Breaking boundaries is what I do.
It is tiring and never ending work.
As I walk back to my place, removing the glitter from my nails,
I realized that the thought of heaven was never my destination.
It would never accept me, and if it didn't let me in
is heaven worth picturing as home?

Being home is two things:
Familiarity and security.

Being inside his arms, using them as my shield;
a castle impenetrable from attacks physical or emotional,
the heave of his hairy chest comforting as I nudge deeper into him
was a physical place of familiarity and security.

Hearing Español, mi primer lenguaje, the one that mi mamá me enseño,
thinking in Spanish, letting my culture flow through food and dance,
the exclusion of the English-natives
for a brief second as a form of decolonization,
los pensamientos, the Spanish thoughts cultivating in my head
is a mental state of home.

Heaven was idealized in my family as an ending destination,
the home of all homes.
Home is not a destination.
It is moveable and ever changing,
it is here,
and heaven is not worth calling home.

THEY SENT ME TO HELL, SHE SENT ME TO HEAVEN

JOSEPHINE JAEL JIMENEZ

My parents didn't raise me to change my mind. They raised me to follow God and the people who claim to love him more than I do blindly, with no doubts or burning questions taking up space in my mind where the faith it supposed to live inside me. My parents raised me to believe like them.

But I don't.

I remember sitting in Sunday School after we finished singing just the right songs to please God. I remember the doors of the sanctuary closing behind me as I went off to be with the people my own age and learn the same stories I've heard my whole life. Over and over again, the same message replayed in my mind. It went something like this:

Are they fucking with us?

Maybe I didn't curse as a child, but the sentiment was the same. My imagination ran wild with visions of adults sitting behind those closed doors, erupting with laughter as soon as they were shut. We've fooled them again, everybody. These kids don't suspect a thing. One more week of them believing in a God we told them to believe in.

I knew that wasn't true, I knew it wasn't all an elaborate ruse to get us kids to believe in something they themselves didn't, but I thought about that almost every Sunday for a long time.

After a while, I stopped going to church with my parents. I couldn't stomach it anymore. None of it was what I believed, not really. My heart couldn't love a God who threatened Hell at every turn. My self-esteem couldn't handle the adults commenting on the way I looked or the things I said I wanted to be. Truthfully, my ego was too big to be sitting in a building with people who deep down didn't like who I was or where I wanted to go in life. My dreams were bigger than the ones allowed in the walls of that church. So I left.

But I didn't realize that until much later. At the time, I just left because it felt right. Not going to church felt better than being in church. I loved God more when I wasn't there, loved myself and my neighbor more, too.

There was one night where everyone was kicked out of the church building because a young woman was possessed. I remember that so clearly and maybe it didn't happen this way, but I still see it replay like this in my mind. Everyone filed out neatly like it wasn't the most awful sounding thing in the world and a group of men stayed behind. Behind those closed doors, these men were exorcising a demon out of a young woman, that wasn't kept from me or anyone else. It wasn't ideal, but it wasn't the most offensive situation. Just another day in pentecostal Christianity.

Some came out and said it was terrifying, others didn't say anything, like it was just another day on the job. Thinking about it years later, I only pray that it really was a demon inside that young woman. I pray they didn't misdiagnose something worse to stroke their religious egos and I hate that I think about it that way, that these men would do that. But they would.

There were hundreds of prayer nights that went late into the evening, even more weekends confined to this building and just a few less nights of music rehearsals you had to show up to if you even had an ounce of talent. My whole life was expected to be wrapped up in this church, but I don't remember it being encouraged to be wrapped up in God the same way.

My parents left that church eventually and we've only ever gone back for funerals. Most people we knew left after a while, too.

The last time I stepped foot in that building, I roamed into every door, every Sunday school room. None of them had really changed much since I was a kid. Everything was almost exactly the same as when I sat there thinking my parents were trying to trick me. I needed a cigarette pretty bad after walking through all those doors, but I knew better than to smoke in front of the same people I grew up with in that building. I knew what they would say.

I was never going to be the good little Christian girl they wanted me to be. Never ever was I going to live up to the reputation my parents made for themselves there. My clothes were never going to be normal, my words were never going to be quiet and sweet. These tattoos and beers and cigarettes all damned me to Hell a long time ago.

It took a while after I left for me to find God, but I found Her. She was in the arms of people who liked me the way I am, in the hearts of people who didn't agree with everything I said, but respected my humanity anyway. God granted me an education where I could make my own decisions and cultivate my own beliefs. They're not the beliefs of my father, but they leave room for me to think that the difference is okay. It makes life more interesting.

My God taught me that it's okay to evolve, but it's not okay to be stuck being someone I am not. She only loves me when I am who She made me to be. Whether they wanted to or not, these people kept sending me straight to Hell. But my God sent me to myself.

Photograph c/o Josephine Jael Jimenez

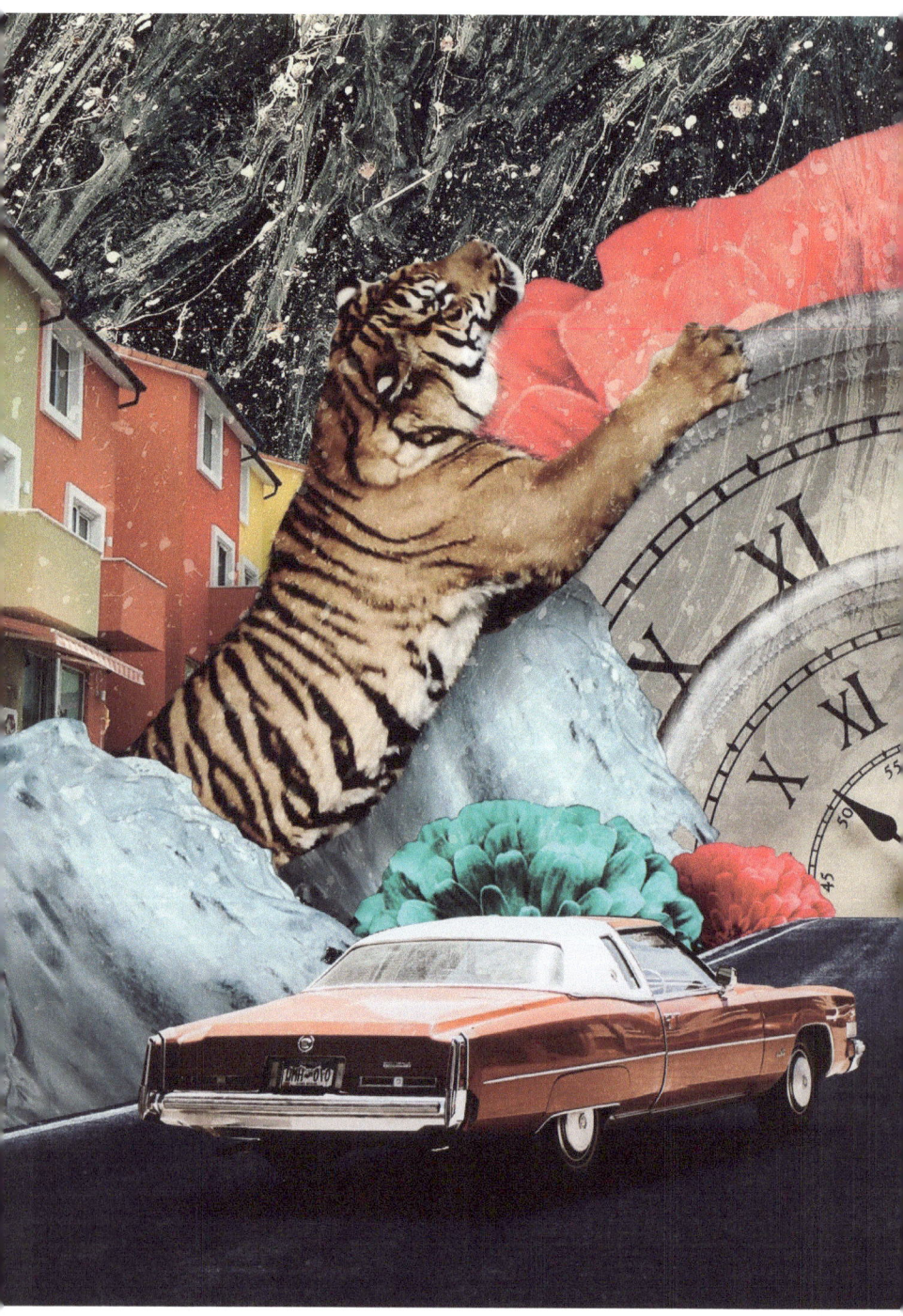

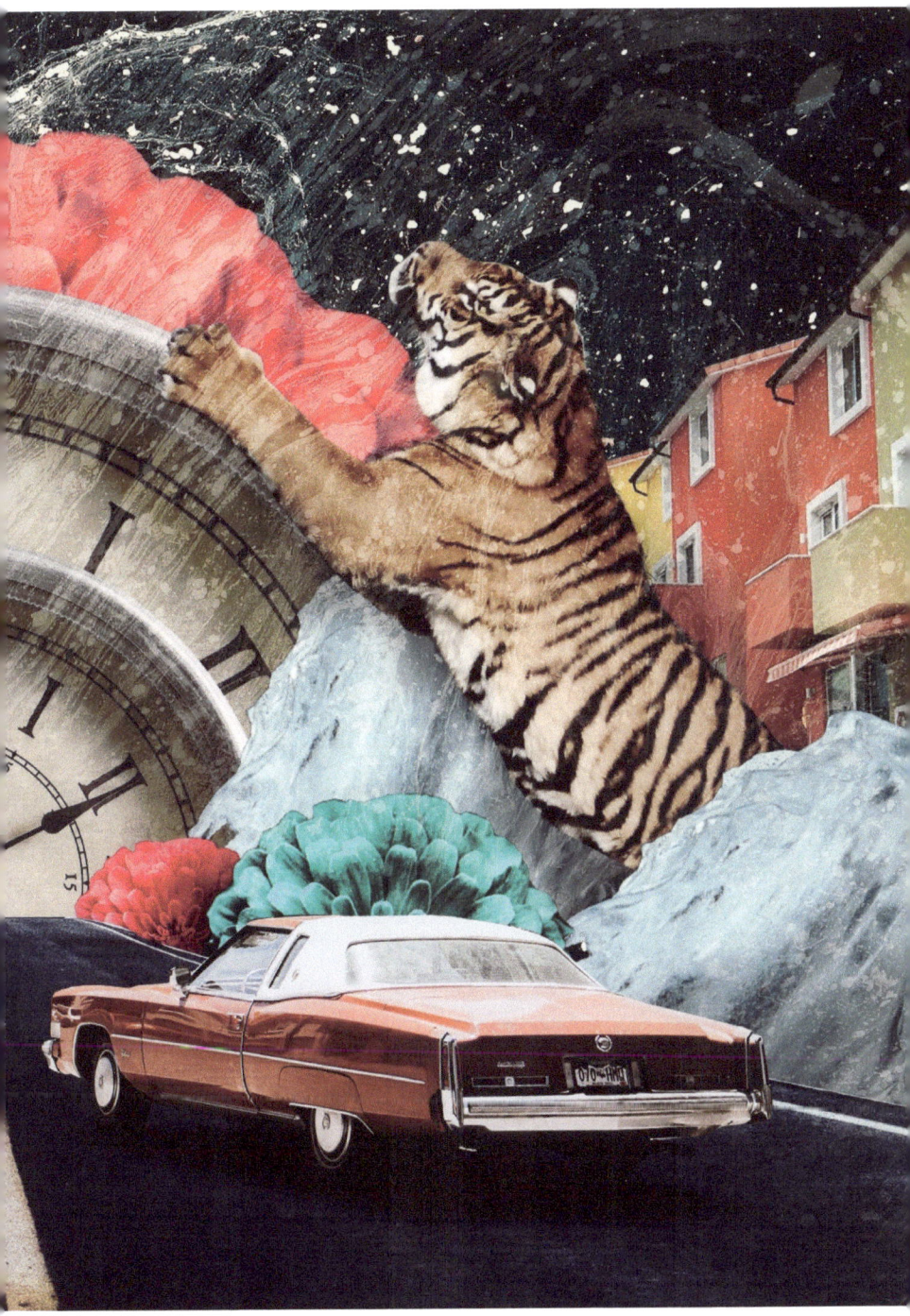

ANCIENT TIGER

BRENDA HERNÁNDEZ JAIMES

The orange ogre forgot that the stolen land birthed strong and fierce tigers that abandoned their fear to strike back. These majestic creatures have roamed these lands before red capped men and women built their shiny mountains.

These venomous beings had forgotten that these stunning tigers are the real king and queen of the jungle. They had rejected the reality and pillage all the treasures that these beautiful creatures held dear.

In spite of the extensive and bloody torture that these creatures faced in the hands of these red beasts, the queens and kings of the jungle have awoken from the slumber that had been imposed on them.

The plights that the ancient tigers have faced awoke a deep anger in their cubs. Enough was enough. Their deep roar shook the repulsive ogres, but didn't stop them from their atrocious actions.

A tiger's bite is deadly and the time is near to taste blood so sweet. This is not revenge. This is defense. The ogres should have known to steer clear of the royal creatures of these stolen lands.

REJECTED 03
Digital Collage *by Sophie Cowell* (previous page)

MAKING ROOM

EVAN BLACK

Now that you
        have faded away
                I feel as if I can
                        take up space
                                in my own heart.

DON'T BE FOOLED. LOVE WILL <u>ALWAYS</u> LEAVE YOU.

ASÍ TU ME MATAS

REBEKAH C. GUERRA

La manera en que me miras, como si fuera yo un espejo.
Tú estás desligado de la realidad,
demasiado distanciado de la fragilidad de la existencia.
Existencia es solo lo que es, algo tan simple pero tan lleno de oscuridad.
Los demonios que te matan son los mismos pensamientos
que tú decides entretener.
Sus canciones mórbidas suenan como poesías a tus oídos muertos.

How do I get rid of the hurt
This pain that beats inside
That I carry with me in stride
That I can't seem to hide
From.
How do I forget everything
The love the hate
All of it
How do I get over this
I want to push my body
Til it trembles with exhaustion
As I throw myself on my bed to sleep
But that eludes me
I don't find a blissful rest
But a torment
Of memories
Bad and good
Well they might as well all be bad
For all the hurt they cause me
His beautiful face
Us together intertwined
Holding hands til the end of time
Then I wake
With a hole in my heart
As I look around my solitary room
My head filled with a never ending gloom
That brings me lower than I've ever felt
That makes me want to lay
And stay
And not do anything
To just give up
To go into the light
With no regrets in sight
My mind and heart are tormented
My soul is becoming shadowed and demented.
I don't see a way out.
I was used, mentally abused
Pushed to believe I was nobody
Nothing
And still I loved
And still I do
...
I love you
But fuck you.

MELISSA ARELLANO

UNTITLED
Digital Illustration *by Bryn Riihimaki*

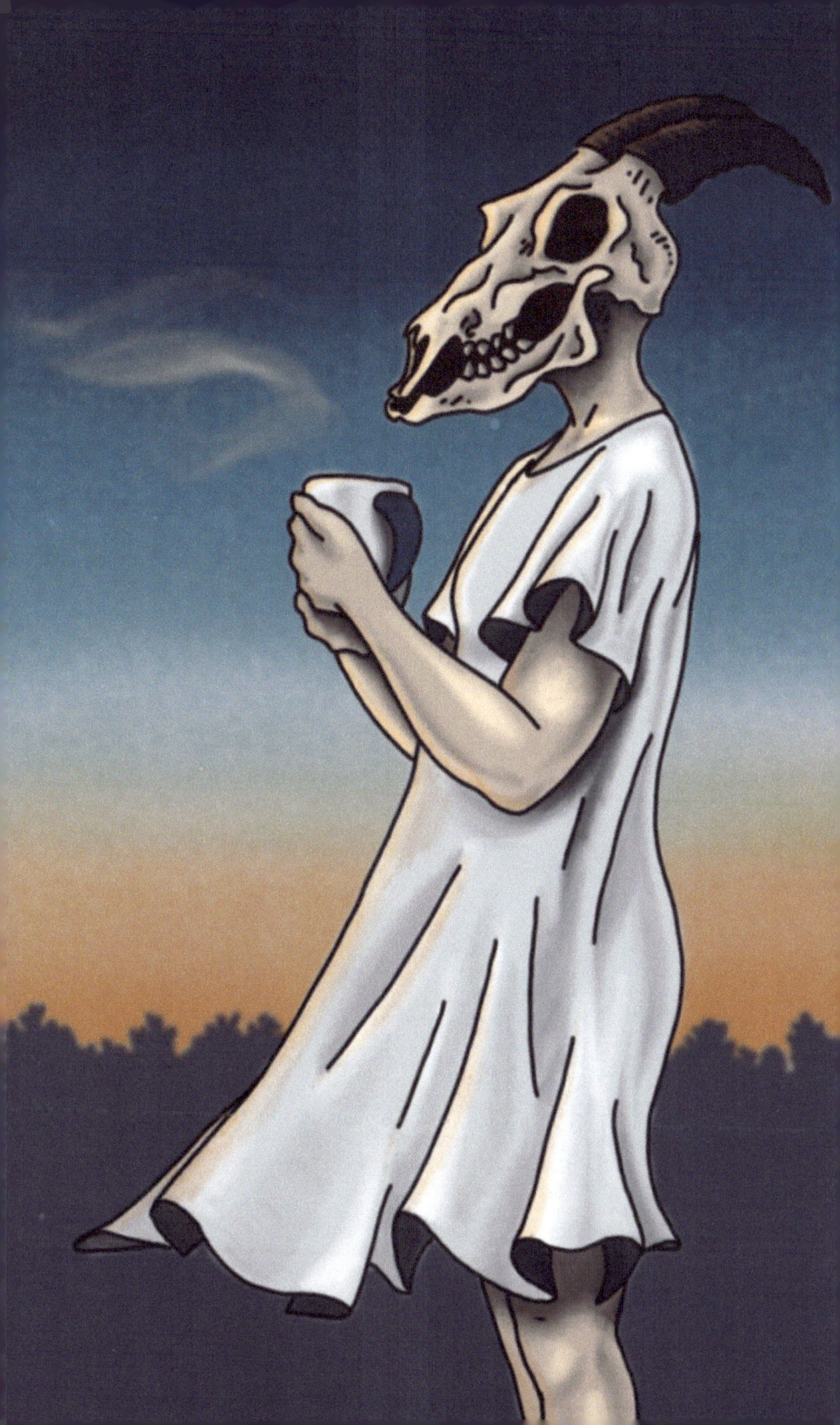

PRINCIPITO

CARLOS GARCÍA LEÓN

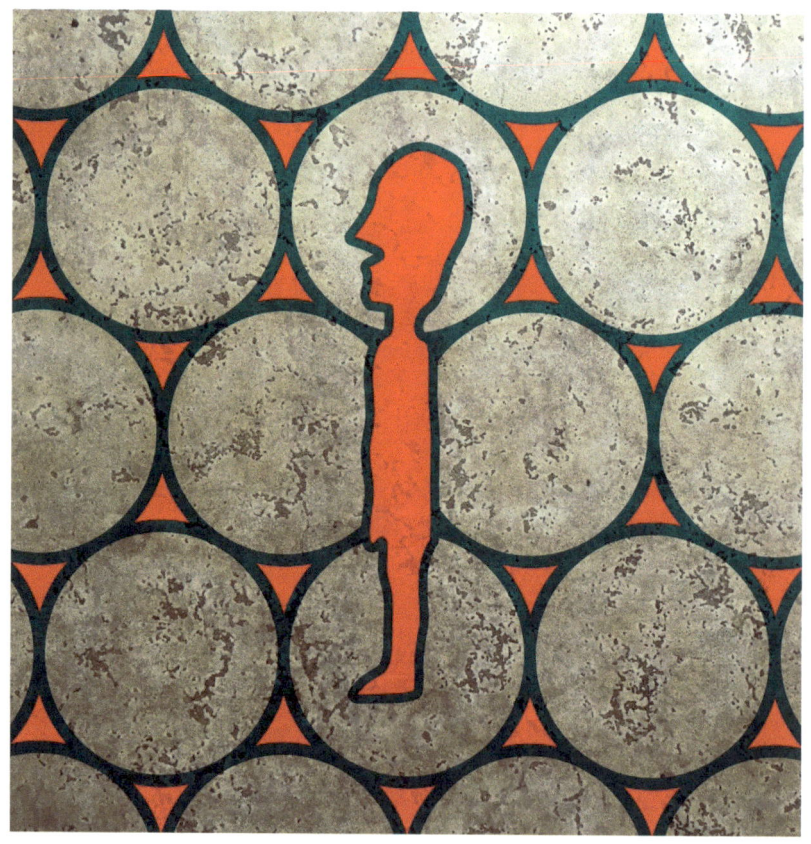

MINSTREL
Digital Illustration *by Evan Black*

I am a prince –
always wanted to be royalty –
in my household.

I was wanted,
begged, prayed, and asked for.
Being the first-born son of my parents,
I was loved, like the sun in the sky
and the moon's reflection of the light.

My brother came later.
He was not a prince,
but he grew up like one and trained as a knight.

My father and his knight were a lot a like
in taste and personality.
Loved the hunt of the soccer ball, the fights to be emotionless,
learning things that I was not asked to participate in...

Excluding me from the glass roundtable mi mamá bought
as we ate el mole poblano that held us at the table.

This prince wanted to fight,
wanted to wield a sword and shield,
wanted to be outside the room where I hid
when trouble came.

Why was I shielded from everything?
Was it because of love?
It's not love when I feel useless in tough situations
mocked at for volunteering,
ignored and send away to get the knight for help...

The kingdom called my house was founded
on misogyny, machismo, and mole poblano.
When I left, I only missed el mole

I founded my own kingdom,
my chosen roundtable is family.
I still don't know how to fight with a sword,
but I'll just crush you with self-taught castlemade mole.

OUR PEOPLE

ANABEL OROZCO
@belle_orozco21

ANNETTE CORTEZ
@annett_ers

BRENDA DESHAZER
@bee.andi

BRENDA HERNÁNDEZ JAIMES
@bren_jai
brenjai.com

BRYN RIIHIMAKI
@itsjustbryn

CARLOS GARCIA LEÓN
@cgarcia_leon

CHASE GOLDSMITH

EVAN BLACK
@evanisthenewblack
evanvblack.com

EROS PURIZAGA
@mynameiseros

JOSEPH A. REYES
@joeykangarooooo

JOSEPHINE JAEL JIMENEZ
@josietakestheworld
josietakestheworld.com

LORRAINE RUMSON
@its.lorraining

MELISSA ARELLANO
@melsartpetals

NICK BLACK
@blacknick
nickrblack.com

REBEKAH C. GUERRA
rebekahguerra.com

YOUNG IGNORANTES
@youngignorantes
youngignorantes.com